Love
POTIONS

"Mix me a potion
That my love shall partake
Once taken my love
Will never forsake."

Love
POTIONS

JULIA JONES
and
KENNETH AMES

With Photography by
DEREK HARRIS

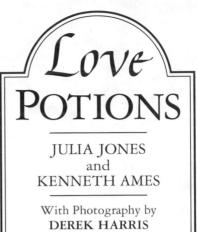

LONGMEADOW
P R E S S

ACKNOWLEDGEMENTS

The authors and photographer would like to thank the following for their help in producing this book:

Mary Fry, Fulbeck Hall, Lincs; G. Baldwin & Co, Medical Herbalists, 171 Walworth Road, London, SE17 1RW; Jasmin Dallaway, Midland Herb Supply Co Ltd., 1a Formans Trading Estate, Pentos Drive, Sparkhill, Birmingham B11 3TA; Pamela Harper; Barbara Deer.

The authors and photographer have made every effort to obtain copyright permission where necessary on the text and items used in this book. However, should an oversight have been made, this will be corrected in the next edition in this series.

Text © 1992 Hidden Treasures
Photographs © 1992 Derek Harris

Published by Longmeadow Press,
201 High Ridge Road,
Stamford, CT. 06904

Cover and interior design by Vic Giolitto.

ISBN 0 681 41771 4

Printed in Hong Kong.

First Edition

0 9 8 7 6 5 4 3 2 1

CONTENTS

The Valentine Cup
The Spirit of Love
Welcomes you all

Amor Vincit Omnia! - Love Conquers All!

POTION: a medicine based on ingredients of a particular character. From the Latin "potio" - a drink or poisonous draught.

Love potions - the very words stir the imagination. Their origins are shrouded in an ancient mystery, which stems from the time when man was in closer touch with nature.

Their use was widespread and their ingredients many and varied. In this book we have chosen to include those that are readily available to recreate the potions of the past.

Number 1
A BLEND OF HERBS AND SPICES

In medieval times, the pretty blue-flowered herb "borage" was used a "pep" pill to lift flagging spirits and to lighten the heart. Even its name testifies to its powers. "Borrach" is a Celtic word for courage. It was said to induce a state of euphoria, which the drinker would attribute to the company, rather than to the drink!

INGREDIENTS
100g/4oz toasted bread
150g/6oz sugar
1 sugar lump saturated with orange-flower essence
¹/4 tsp nutmeg
¹/4 tsp cinnamon
¹/4 tsp ginger
1 litre/2 pints brown ale
¹/2 litre/1 pint mead
10–12 borage flowers

METHOD
Put the toasted bread into a bowl, add the sugar and sugar lump saturated with orange-flower essence. Add nutmeg and mix in the ground cinnamon and ginger. Pour in brown ale and mead. Stir well and sprinkle with flowers. Leave to stand for one hour. Strain and serve.

Partake of this with the object of your desires, but not too liberally!

Mead has for centuries been known as the honeymoon drink.

"But of all the lunar things that change
The one that shows most fickle and strange
And takes the most eccentric range
Is the moon - so called - of honey."

THOMAS HOOD

In former times, honeyed wines were taken as an aphrodisiac during the first month of marriage.

"Ah, drink me up
That I may be
Within your cup
Like a mystery,
Like wine that is still
In ecstasy.

Glimmering still
In ecstasy
Commingled wines
Of you and me
In one fulfil
The mystery."

D. H. LAWRENCE
"The Mystery"

Love
POTIONS

Number 2
HONEY AND FLOWERS

Pansies have always been associated with love. Their heart-shaped leaves were a sure sign to the lovelorn of the 17th century that this flower could cure a broken heart. In earlier centuries, the Celts made a tea from dried pansy leaves and used this as a love potion.

INGREDIENTS
2 tsp dried heartsease
2-3 cloves
1 tblspn clear honey
$^1/_4$ litre/$^1/_2$ pint red wine

METHOD
Place the herbs and spices into a warm jug and cover with a little boiling water. Allow to infuse for 10 minutes. Strain and sweeten with 1 tablespoon of clear honey. Add $^1/_4$ litre/$^1/_2$ pint red wine and warm gently. Serve hot.

According to legend, pansies were once only white. However, one day Cupid, the Roman God of Love, shot an arrow which happened to hit a nearby flower. From that day onwards the pansy changed its colour to purples and yellows, wounded by Love and bearing its magical powers.

"Yet mark'd I where the bolt of Cupid fell,
It fell upon a little western flower,
Before milk-white, now purple with
love's wound,
And maidens call it Love-in-Idleness.
Fetch me that flower - the herb I showed
thee once;
The juice of it on sleeping eyelids laid
Will make a man or woman, madly dote
Upon the next live creature that it sees."

WILLIAM SHAKESPEARE
"A Midsummer Night's Dream"

"Sweet flowers that in the still hour grew
We'll take them home, nor shake off the
bright dew."

JOHN CLARE
"Mary"

*"I learned my fate but lately, when upon my bethinking
me whether you loved me, not even did the poppy coming
in contact make a sound, but withered away just so
upon my soft arm."*

THEOCRITUS,
"The Third Idyll"

Number 3

RED WINE AND SWEET SPICES

Carnations have long been associated with weddings. Their flowers were often used to spice the wine given to brides after the wedding ceremony, in the belief that they were a powerful aphrodisiac. In Italy today, the carnation is still a symbol of ardent love. So why not try this modern interpretation of a very old love potion?

INGREDIENTS
12^1/$_2$g/^{1}/$_2$oz cinnamon
12^1/$_2$g/^{1}/$_2$oz ginger
7g/^{1}/$_4$oz cloves
^{1}/$_2$kg/1lb soft brown sugar
1 litre/2 pints red burgundy wine
petals from two clove carnations

METHOD
Put all the ingredients into a large pan and heat slowly, stirring until the sugar dissolves. Strain and bottle.

Given to a loved one, this was guaranteed to bring success!

"Bring carnations and 'sops in wine' worn of paramours."

EDMUND SPENSER

"Sops in wine" was an Elizabethan name for "pinks". The pink was worn as an indication to possible suitors that the wearer's affections were already taken.

"And now St Agnes, play thy part
And send to me mine own sweetheart
And show to me such happy bliss
This night of him to have a kiss!"

"Agnes sweet, Agnes fair
Hither, hither now repair
Bonny Agnes, let me see
The lad who is to marry me."

TRADITIONAL

On the 20th January
falls St Agnes' Eve.
St Agnes will intercede
in affairs of the heart.

Number 4

APPLES AND JASMINE

"As one who drinks from a charméd cup
Of foaming, and sparkling, and murmuring
wine,
Whom, a mighty Enchantress filling up,
Invites to love with her kiss divine...."

PERCY BYSSHE SHELLEY
"Music"

INGREDIENTS
1 tsp dried woodruff
$^1/_2$ tsp dried jasmine flowers
$^1/_2$ litre/1 pint clear apple juice
1 red skinned apple

METHOD
Sprinkle the herbs and flowers into $^1/_8$ litre/
$^1/_4$ pint of clear apple juice, and chill for 2 hours.
Strain and stir in the remaining juice.
Just before serving add a slice of apple to
each glass.

The apple was the "forbidden fruit" from the tree of
knowledge, with which Eve tempted Adam.

ALEXIS: *"They have invented a philtre, which, if report may be believed, is simply infallible. I intend to distribute it through the village, and within half an hour of my doing so, there will not be an adult in the place, who will not have learnt the secret of pure and lasting happiness."*

W.S. GILBERT
"The Sorcerer"

"Let us twine like amorous trees."

"This love it was a bud
And a secret known to me
Like a flower within a wood
Like a nest within a tree."

JOHN CLARE
"Love's Pain"

"You, Helen, who see the stars
As mistletoe berries burning in a black tree,
You surely, seeing I am a bowl of kisses,
Should put your mouth to mine and
drink of me."

D. H. LAWRENCE
"The Appeal"

Love POTIONS

Number 5
CHAMPAGNE AND STRAWBERRIES

Champagne and strawberries have long had the reputation, when combined, of being a powerful aphrodisiac. With the added benefit of verbena, this drink provides a very effective love potion.

> "Wine comes in at the mouth
> And love comes in at the eye;
> That's all we know for truth
> Before we grow old and die.
> I lift the glass to my mouth,
> I look at you, and I sigh."

W. B. YEATS
"A Drinking Song"

INGREDIENTS
1 tsp scented rose geranium leaves
1 tsp lemon verbena leaves
1 bottle sweet white wine
100g/4oz strawberries
1 bottle soda water or champagne

Put the leaves into a jug and pour on the wine.
Leave at room temperature for at least four hours.
Strain and add sliced strawberries. Chill for 30
minutes. Just before serving pour in chilled soda
water or champagne.

Verbena was used in many ways as an aphrodisiac.
Pillows were stuffed with dried verbena leaves and
placed on marriage beds, and its blossoms strewn
on the floor of the bridal chamber.

A bowl of pot-pourri containing verbena placed
on a table near the door of your bedroom, being
stirred with the fourth finger of the left hand on
entering the room, is said to induce a mood
of love.

"And, when at length in that strange ecstasy
The heavy sigh will start
There rains upon my heart
A love so pure and fine
That I say: 'Lady, I am wholly thine.'"

DANTE GABRIEL ROSSETTI

"I prithee send me back my heart,
Since I cannot have thine
For if from yours you will not part
Why then should'st thou have mine?"

SIR JOHN SUCKLING

Number 6

BRANDY AND BORAGE

The efficacy of this potion relies on the combination of brandy and sherry with the exhilarating properties of borage. For the best results it should be used very sparingly.

INGREDIENTS
1 lemon
1 litre/2 pints dry cider
25g/1oz fresh borage leaves
¹/₂ litre/1 pint orange juice
¹/₂ cup sherry
¹/₂ cup brandy
50g/2oz sugar
soda water to taste

METHOD
Finely peel the lemon and prick all over with a fork. Put into a jug and pour in the cider. Then add chopped borage leaves. Chill for 4 hours. Add orange juice, sherry, brandy and sugar, stirring well.

Just before serving, remove lemon and add soda water to taste.

"Here in the garden of our first embrace,
We lost our hearts
And bless'd this place."

"Iseult's mother gathered herbs and flowers and roots
and steeped them in wine, and brewed a potion of might,
and having done so, said, 'Take then this pitcher and
remember well my words. Hide it so that no eye shall
see, no lip go near it.... For this is its power: they who
drink of it together love each other with every single
sense and with their every thought, forever, in life and
in death.'"

"TRISTAN AND ISEULT"
from the translation by
Hilaire Belloc

"'Twas the maiden's matchless beauty
That drew my heart a-nigh;
Not the fern-root potion,
But the glance of her blue eye."

ANON.

Number 7

VANILLA AND JASMINE

The warm, spicy and slightly heady scent of cinnamon bark, combined with the perfume of jasmine and vanilla, makes this potion perfect for serving on a chill winter's evening.

INGREDIENTS
2 tsp dried jasmine flowers
1/2 vanilla pod
2–3 cloves
1/2 stick cinnamon
1/4 litre/1/2 pint red wine
honey (optional)

METHOD
Place the flowers, vanilla pod, cloves and cinnamon into a warmed jug. Cover with a little boiling water and allow to infuse for 10 minutes.

Strain and add 1/4 litre/1/2 pint red wine. Sweeten with a little honey to taste if required. Warm gently and serve.

"Cupid, if storying Legends tell aright,
Once fram'd a rich Elixir of Delight.
A chalice o'er love-kindled flames he fix'd,
And in it Nectar and Ambrosia mix'd,
With these the magic dews, which
Evening brings
brush'd from the Idalian star by faery wings:
Each tender pledge of Sacred Faith he join'd
Each gentler Pleasure of th' unspotted mind —"

SAMUEL TAYLOR COLERIDGE
"Kisses"

Bacchus, Roman God
of Wine, was said
to have drunk from
beechwood bowls!

*Amethysts were reputed to be an antidote to love potions
and charms. They offered sure protection when steeped in
the suspect wine.*

One day Bacchus threw a young woman to the lions.
Venus turned her into a column of quartz and the
remorseful god poured wine over this, giving it the
purple of amethyst.

Love
POTIONS

Number 8
FINE WINE AND FLOWERS

According to the Greeks of ancient times, the use of the "warming" herbs rosemary and feverfew in this potion was certain to inflame the passion of any young man to whom it was served. These herbs were said to be particularly effective when steeped in vintage wine.

"And, therefore, if love be a fire
Then he shall burn me up.
If love be water out of the mire,
Then I will be the cup."

GEORGE AUGUSTUS SIMCOX
"Love's Votary"

INGREDIENTS
1 bottle vintage claret
2 tsp dried or fresh rosemary flowers
1 tsp dried or fresh chopped violet leaves

METHOD
Pour the claret into a jug and add the rosemary flowers and chopped leaves. Stand at room temperature for 2 hours. Strain into a decanter and serve.

*"Teach me where that wondrous
Mandrake grows,
Whose magic root, torn from the earth
with groans,
At midnight hour, can scare the fiends away,
And make the mind prolific in its fancies!"*

HENRY WADSWORTH LONGFELLOW

42

"He is handsome
He is shy
And I'll love him
Till I die."

Number 9

A FLOWER-LACED
SUMMER CUP

The pot marigold flowers used in this recipe were considered a splendid aphrodisiac which would also give the drinker the power to see fairies! And marjoram was said to "ease the troubles of such that are given to much sighing".

INGREDIENTS
1 tsp dried lavender flowers
1/2 tsp dried marjoram leaves
1 tsp fresh marigold petals
1 bottle of soda water
slices of lemon

METHOD
Tip the flowers and leaves into the bottle of soda water. Replace cap and shake gently. Leave in the refrigerator for 24 hours. Strain and serve with ice and lemon.

Alternatively, plain mineral water may be substituted and the strained potion used to make tea or coffee!

To keep the attention of a lover, bedlinen
should be perfumed with marjoram.
According to Virgil, when Venus carried off
Ascanius she laid him on a bed of marjoram.

"Come lover, come lad
And make my heart glad
For a husband I'll have
For good or for bad."

TRADITIONAL

45

"And break upon thee, bathing, in
woody place alone,
And catch thee to my saddle and ride
o'er stream and stone,
And press thee well, and kiss thee well,
and never speak a word,
Till thou hast yielded up,
The margin of love's cup."

THOMAS LOVELL BEDDOES
"Love-in-Idleness"

Number 10
A WARMING SPICED WINE

As long ago as 40 AD, the Romans served this honeyed wine at banquets to increase desire. They were advised that its best effect was achieved when taken in small quantities.

INGREDIENTS
1 bottle of white wine
1 tblspn honey
pinch of freshly ground black pepper
pinch of saffron
1 tsp dried red tulip flowers
pinch of cinnamon
2 chopped dates

METHOD
Put the wine into a saucepan and stir in the honey. Heat slowly, stirring continuously until hot. Add pepper, saffron, tulip flowers and cinnamon. Put in the chopped dates and simmer for 15 minutes. Strain and serve.

"The wine is warm in the hearth;
The flickers come and go.
I will warm your limbs with kisses
Until they glow."

D. H. LAWRENCE
"December Night"

"Why we love and why we hate
Is not granted us to know;
Random chance, or wilful fate,
Guides the shaft from Cupid's bow."

AMBROSE PHILIPS

"As lately I a garland bound,
'Mongst roses I there Cupid found;
I took him, put him in my cup,
And drunk with wine, I drank him up.
Hence then it is that my poor breast
Could never since find any rest."

ROBERT HERRICK
"Upon Cupid"

"Like a sleeper
Half dreaming
I slumbered my time
All wonders were hidden from view
Now waken'd
Alive
I'm breathless, entranc'd
By the beauty I now see in you."

Love
POTIONS

Number 11

SHERRY SPIKED WITH SAFFRON

"Could you not drink her gaze like wine?"

DANTE GABRIEL ROSSETTI
"The Card-dealer"

INGREDIENTS
2 tsps dried peony flowers
2 tsps dried rose petals
pinch of saffron
1 bottle dry sherry

METHOD
Crush the peony flowers and rose petals and add
with the saffron to a bottle of dry sherry. Leave for
about a week in a cool place. Strain and
serve chilled.

According to Eastern sources, the combination of
peony flowers and rose petals made a wonderful
love potion, which would assure success. The
secret was to adminster little and often to the
object of one's desires.

Angus, the ancient Celtic God of Love and
Dalliance, bestowed kisses which turned into
invisible, love-whispering birds. It was said that
the music of his harp was so sweet that all who
heard it would become entranced.

The Apsaras were the enchanting nymphs of
India's heaven. These fairy-like beings were
extremely beautiful and tempting and said to
number thirty-five million!

Number 12

A COUNTRY RECIPE

The ingredients for this potion were highly regarded for their love-inducing properties and they were combined with light ale in rural areas to entice the local boys.

INGREDIENTS
2 pints light ale
2 tsps dried borage
1 tsp dried woodruff
1 tsp dried chervil

METHOD
Pour the ale into a jug and stir in dried herbs.
Leave at room temperature for 2 hours. Strain,
chill and serve.

"Straight to the 'pothecary's shop I went,
And in Love-Powder all my money spent;
Behap what will, next Sunday after prayers,
When to the alehouse Lubberkin repairs
These golden flies into his mug I'll throw
And soon the swain with fervent love
shall glow."

JOHN GAY
"The Shepherd's Week"

"Among thy fancies tell me this,
What is the thing we call a kiss?"

"'Tis twelve, I think
And at this mystic hour
The magic drink
Should manifest its power
Oh slumberous forms,
How little have ye guessed
The fire that warms
Each apathetic breast."

W.S. GILBERT
"The Sorcerer"

And finally, should you need an antidote to love, poppy seeds were said to provide the answer. A teaspoon of these should be chewed slowly from time to time to ease the pains of love.